# YOUR COMPLETE LEO 2024 PERSONAL HOROSCOPE

Monthly Astrological Prediction Forecast Readings of Every Zodiac Astrology Sun Star Signs- Love, Romance, Money, Finances, Career, Health, Travel, Spirituality.

Iris Quinn

Alpha Zuriel Publishing

Copyright © 2023 by **Iris Quinn**

All rights reserved. No part of this publication may be reproduced, distributed or transmitted in any form or by any means, without prior written permission.

**Alpha Zuriel Publishing
United States.**

The content contained within this book may not be reproduced, duplicated or transmitted without direct written permission from the author or the publisher.
Under no circumstances will any blame or legal responsibility be held against the publisher, or author, for any damages, reparation, or monetary loss due to the information contained within this book; either directly or indirectly.

Legal Notice:
This book is copyright protected. This book is only for personal use. You cannot amend, distribute, sell, use, quote or paraphrase any part, or the content within this book, without the consent of the author or publisher.

Disclaimer Notice:
Please note the information contained within this document is for educational and entertainment purposes only. All effort has been executed to present accurate, up to date, and reliable, complete information. No warranties of any kind are declared or implied. Readers acknowledge that the author is not engaging in the rendering of legal, financial, medical or professional advice.

**Your Complete Leo 2024 Personal Horoscope/ Iris Quinn**. -- 1st ed.

*"In the dance of the planets, we find the rhythms of life. Astrology reminds us that we are all connected to the greater universe, and our actions have ripple effects throughout the cosmos."*
— IRIS QUINN

# CONTENTS

- LEO PROFILE .......................................................... 1
- PERSONALITY OF LEO ........................................ 5
- WEAKNESSES OF LEO ........................................ 7
- RELATIONSHIP COMPATIBILITY WITH LEO 9
- LOVE AND PASSION ......................................... 17
- MARRIAGE .......................................................... 20
- LEO 2024 HOROSCOPE ...................................... 23
  - Overview Leo 2024 ............................................ 23
  - January 2024 ...................................................... 27
  - February 2024 .................................................... 33
  - March 2024 ........................................................ 39
  - April 2024 .......................................................... 44
  - May 2024 ........................................................... 49
  - June 2024 ........................................................... 55
  - July 2024 ........................................................... 60
  - August 2024 ...................................................... 65
  - September 2024 ................................................. 70
  - October 2024 ..................................................... 75
  - November 2024 ................................................. 80
  - December 2024 .................................................. 85

1 · COMPLETE LEO 2024 PERSONAL HOROSCOPE

CHAPTER ONE

# LEO PROFILE

- Constellation: Leo
- Zodiac Symbol: The Lion
- Date: July 23 - August 22
- Element: Fire
- Ruling Planet: Sun
- Career Planet: Sun
- Love Planet: Sun
- Money Planet: Sun
- Planet of Fun, Entertainment, Creativity, and Speculations: Jupiter
- Planet of Health and Work: Mercury
- Planet of Home and Family Life: Moon
- Planet of Spirituality: Neptune
- Planet of Travel, Education, Religion, and Philosophy: Mars

Leo Colors:
- Colors: Gold, Orange

- Colors that promote love, romance, and social harmony: Red, Pink
- Color that promotes earning power: Yellow

- Gem: Ruby
- Metals: Gold, Brass
- Scent: Citrus
- Birthstone: Peridot

Leo Qualities:
- Quality: Fixed (Stability)
- Quality most needed for balance: Flexibility.

Leo Virtues:
- Confidence
- Generosity
- Leadership
- Charisma
- Passion

- Deepest Need: Recognition and admiration

Characteristics to Embrace:
- Courage
- Creativity
- Playfulness
- Self-expression

Signs of Greatest Overall Compatibility:
- Aries
- Sagittarius

Signs of Greatest Overall Incompatibility:
- Taurus
- Scorpio

- Sign Most Supportive for Career Advancement: Capricorn
- Sign Most Supportive for Emotional Well-being: Cancer
- Sign Most Supportive Financially: Taurus
- Sign Best for Marriage and/or Partnerships: Libra
- Sign Most Supportive for Creative Projects: Leo
- Best Sign to Have Fun With: Leo

Signs Most Supportive in Spiritual Matters:
- Sagittarius
- Pisces

Best Day of the Week: Sunday

## LEO TRAITS

- Confident and charismatic
- Natural born leaders
- Passionate and expressive
- Generous and giving
- Playful and fun-loving
- Creative and artistic
- Strong sense of self
- Command attention and admiration
- Loyal and devoted
- Determined and ambitious
- Warm-hearted and affectionate
- Optimistic and enthusiastic
- Dramatic and theatrical
- Courageous and fearless
- Energetic and vibrant
- Inspiring and influential

## PERSONALITY OF LEO

In the realm of personality, Leos are a force to be reckoned with. They possess a unique blend of courage, warmth, and love that radiates from their very being. Like a majestic lion, they exude a regal aura and command attention wherever they go.

Leos are born entertainers, graced with the dramatic flair of a seasoned performer and the natural charisma of a born leader. They have a way with words that can captivate audiences, effortlessly captivating them with their eloquence and charm. No matter the topic at hand, Leos can speak with confidence and conviction, making even the most complex subjects seem accessible and fascinating.

At the core of their being, Leos are driven by their passionate hearts. They wholeheartedly invest themselves in everything they undertake, infusing their endeavors with enthusiasm and determination. They trust their instincts and have a natural knack for making bold decisions. Their actions flow with ease and authenticity, drawing others in with their genuine and magnetic presence.

While Leos may seem self-assured and invincible, they possess an insatiable need for validation and admiration. They thrive on the recognition and applause of others, finding fulfillment in the spotlight. However, beneath their confident exterior, Leos can also harbor vulnerabilities. They may use their fiery temper as a shield, protecting themselves from their deepest insecurities and fears of dependence. Their desire to be seen as strong stems from a fear of exposing their inner vulnerabilities, relying on others, and feeling incomplete.

In the grand tapestry of personality, Leos shine as radiant stars, illuminating the world with their captivating presence. They are driven by an innate desire to be seen and acknowledged, fueling their relentless pursuit of success and recognition. Yet, amidst their quest for greatness, Leos also long for genuine connection and acceptance, yearning to find a sense of wholeness and purpose.

## WEAKNESSES OF LEO

The negative aspects of a Leo emerge when their favorable and outstanding personality traits become Leos, like any other zodiac sign, possess their own set of weaknesses that they should be mindful of:

In their pursuit of recognition and admiration, Leos may sometimes come across as self-centered or overly focused on themselves. Their inherent confidence and desire for attention can overshadow the needs and perspectives of others.

Their strong-willed nature can also manifest as stubbornness, making it challenging for Leos to accept differing opinions or admit when they are wrong. This inflexibility can lead to conflicts and strained relationships.

As natural leaders, Leos may have a tendency to seek control and dominance, sometimes finding it difficult to share power or compromise. They prefer to be in charge and have things done their way, which can create power struggles and hinder collaborative efforts.

Leos thrive on praise and validation from others, fueling their confidence and drive. However, this constant need for external approval can make them vulnerable to seeking validation at the expense of their own authenticity. They may become overly reliant on others' opinions, fearing criticism or rejection.

Their dramatic nature and intense emotions can sometimes lead to exaggerated reactions and melodrama. Leos may struggle to manage their emotions, resulting in heated conflicts and intense interpersonal dynamics.

Additionally, Leos can be impatient when it comes to achieving their goals. Their drive for success and desire for immediate results can lead to frustration when things don't progress as quickly as they would like.

Awareness of these weaknesses can help Leos navigate their relationships and personal growth with greater self-awareness and understanding. By embracing their strengths and working on these areas of growth, Leos can cultivate more balanced and fulfilling connections with others.

# RELATIONSHIP COMPATIBILITY WITH LEO

Based only on their Sun signs, this is how Leo interacts with others. These are the compatibility interpretations for all 12 potential Leo combinations. This is a limited and insufficient method of determining compatibility.

However, Sun-sign compatibility remains the foundation for overall harmony in a relationship.

The general rule is that yin and yang do not get along. Yin complements yin, and yang complements yang. While yin and yang partnerships can be successful, they require more effort. Earth and water zodiac signs are both Yin. Yang is represented by the fire and air zodiac signs.

Leo (Yang) and Aries (Yang)

When Leo and Aries come together, their shared Yang energy creates a passionate and dynamic connection. They both have a strong desire for adventure, leadership, and excitement. Their relationship is marked by fiery enthusiasm, mutual support, and a shared drive for success. With their vibrant personalities, they encourage each other to take risks, pursue their ambitions, and embrace life's challenges. Their compatibility lies in their shared passion, loyalty, and the ability to fuel each other's desires. Together, they form a power couple that thrives on shared adventures and mutual admiration.

Leo (Yang) and Taurus (Yin)

Leo and Taurus form a complementary partnership where stability and passion harmonize. Taurus' grounded nature provides a solid foundation for Leo's fiery energy. Together, they create a balance of security and excitement, valuing loyalty, romance, and shared values. Taurus' practicality grounds Leo's grand visions, while Leo's warmth and charisma ignite Taurus' sensual nature. They enjoy a deep emotional connection, and their love is built on trust, devotion, and mutual respect. Both signs appreciate the finer things in life and create a luxurious and comfortable environment for their relationship to flourish.

### Leo (Yang) and Gemini (Yang)

The union of Leo and Gemini brings together two energetic and outgoing personalities. They share a love for socializing, intellectual stimulation, and adventure. Their relationship is filled with laughter, creativity, and a constant flow of new experiences. Leo's magnetic charm captivates Gemini, while Gemini's wit and curiosity keep Leo engaged and entertained. They inspire each other to embrace their passions, pursue their interests, and maintain an active social life. Both signs thrive on attention and recognition, making their partnership a vibrant and exciting journey.

### Leo (Yang) and Cancer (Yin)

When Leo and Cancer join forces, they create a nurturing and loving bond. Leo's warmth and passion blend with Cancer's sensitivity and loyalty. They form a strong emotional connection and provide each other with support, affection, and a sense of belonging. Leo's protective nature complements Cancer's need for security, while Cancer's intuitive understanding fulfills Leo's desire for admiration. Together, they create a safe and loving home environment where their love and creativity can flourish. Their shared values of family, loyalty, and emotional depth form the foundation of a lasting and fulfilling partnership.

### Leo (Yang) and Leo (Yang)

When two Leo individuals come together, they create a dynamic and passionate union. They share a love for self-expression, grand gestures, and attention. Their relationship is marked by a fiery and magnetic connection, fueled by their mutual desire to shine and be admired. They understand each other's need for attention and affirmation, supporting and encouraging each other's ambitions. However, their strong personalities can lead to power struggles and clashes of egos. Learning to share the spotlight and balance their individual desires with compromise is crucial for the success of their relationship. When they find the right balance, they create a powerful and radiant partnership that lights up any room they enter.

### Leo (Yang) and Virgo (Yin)

Leo and Virgo bring together confidence and practicality. Leo's vibrant energy is balanced by Virgo's grounded nature. They can support and complement each other, with Leo providing excitement and inspiration, while Virgo offers stability and attention to detail. Leo's enthusiasm helps Virgo come out of their shell, while Virgo's analytical mind helps Leo channel their energy effectively. They can build a solid and harmonious relationship based on trust, respect, and shared goals. Their ability to bring out the best in each other makes them a powerful and balanced couple.

### Leo (Yang) and Libra (Yang)

Leo and Libra form a powerful partnership fueled by mutual respect, admiration, and a shared love for beauty and harmony. Their magnetic personalities and passion for life make them a captivating duo. Together, they create a dynamic and stylish union that thrives on romance, artistry, and social connections. Leo's natural leadership complements Libra's diplomatic skills, allowing them to navigate any situation with grace and charm. They appreciate each other's individuality and support each other's ambitions, creating a harmonious and fulfilling relationship built on mutual admiration and shared values.

### Leo (Yang) and Scorpio (Yin)

When Leo and Scorpio come together, their connection is intense and passionate. Both signs possess strong personalities and a deep desire for loyalty and commitment. Their relationship is marked by emotional depth, shared ambitions, and a strong sexual connection. Leo's magnetic presence ignites Scorpio's intensity, while Scorpio's mysterious nature intrigues and captivates Leo. They challenge each other to grow and evolve, pushing the boundaries of their comfort zones. Trust and open communication are crucial for their relationship to thrive, as both signs have a strong need for honesty and authenticity.

### Leo (Yang) and Sagittarius (Yang)

When Leo and Sagittarius join forces, they ignite a fiery and adventurous connection. They share a zest for life, a thirst for knowledge, and a desire for freedom. Their relationship is characterized by mutual support, exploration, and a shared love for excitement. Leo's charisma and passion complement Sagittarius' adventurous spirit, creating a vibrant and dynamic partnership. They inspire each other to embrace new experiences, chase their dreams, and live life to the fullest. Their relationship is filled with laughter, optimism, and a shared sense of adventure, making them an unstoppable duo.

Leo (Yang) and Capricorn (Yin)

Leo and Capricorn bring together ambition and determination. Leo's enthusiasm and creativity blend with Capricorn's practicality and discipline. They can inspire each other to reach new heights and create a strong foundation for success. Leo's charisma helps Capricorn come out of their shell, while Capricorn's focus and perseverance keep Leo grounded. They share a strong work ethic and a drive for achievement, making them a power couple in both their personal and professional lives. By respecting each other's goals and supporting each other's ambitions, they can create a harmonious and fruitful partnership.

Leo (Yang) and Aquarius (Yang)

The combination of Leo and Aquarius brings together two independent and visionary individuals. They inspire each other to reach new heights, challenge societal norms, and pursue their unique passions. Their connection is marked by intellectual stimulation, mutual admiration, and a shared desire to make a difference in the world. Leo's warmth and creativity complement Aquarius' innovative ideas, creating a partnership that is both exciting and intellectually fulfilling. They support each other's individuality and share a deep respect for personal freedom and expression.

### Leo (Yang) and Pisces (Yin)

Leo and Pisces create a relationship filled with romance, creativity, and emotional depth. Leo's warmth and confidence provide security for Pisces' sensitive nature. They can offer each other support, inspiration, and a sense of magic in their shared experiences. Leo's passion and creativity awaken Pisces' imagination, while Pisces' compassion and intuition bring out the tender side of Leo. They can create a harmonious and soulful partnership where they explore their dreams, express their emotions, and support each other's spiritual growth. Their love is deep, profound, and capable of transcending the ordinary.

## LOVE AND PASSION

When it comes to love and passion, Leo is a force to be reckoned with. Ruled by the radiant Sun, they exude an undeniable magnetism that draws others in. Leos are natural romantics, with an insatiable appetite for love, affection, and grand gestures.

A Leo in love is like a blazing fire, radiating warmth, joy, and a captivating energy. They pour their heart and soul into their relationships, embracing love with a fierce intensity. Their enthusiasm is infectious, as they shower their partner with adoration and make them feel like the center of the universe.

Passion burns bright within the heart of a Leo. They crave a deep and soulful connection, where every touch, every kiss, ignites a spark of electric energy. Their passionate nature is expressed not just physically but also through their zest for life and the way they pursue their dreams and desires.

For Leo, love is an art form, and they are the master artists. They take pleasure in creating romantic experiences that sweep their partner off their feet.

Candlelit dinners, surprise getaways, and heartfelt declarations of love are just a few ways they express their affection.

However, beneath their confident exterior, Leo hides a vulnerable heart. They long for unwavering loyalty and devotion from their partner. They need to be constantly reminded that they are loved, admired, and respected. In return, they offer a love that is fierce and unwavering, a love that will stand the test of time.

Yet, love with a Leo is not without its challenges. Their need for admiration and attention can sometimes border on egoistic. They may demand the spotlight, craving constant validation and adoration. It's crucial for their partner to understand the delicate balance between appreciating their confidence and nurturing their ego.

Leo's fiery nature can also lead to clashes of will and dominance. They are natural-born leaders and desire a partner who can match their strength and ambition. But finding harmony requires mutual respect and a willingness to compromise, allowing both partners to shine in their own unique ways.

In the realm of passion, Leo is a master of seduction. They possess a magnetic charm that entices and captivates their partner. Behind closed doors, their fiery spirit comes alive, bringing a sense of adventure, playfulness, and sensual pleasure. Every touch is filled with intensity, every moment an expression of their deep desire.

Love and passion with a Leo are like a grand performance, an exquisite symphony that evokes raw emotion and leaves an indelible mark on the heart. They long to be the hero or heroine of their partner's story, providing unwavering support, protection, and love.

In the arms of a Leo, you'll find a love that burns brighter than the sun, a passion that knows no bounds. Their warmth, generosity, and devotion create a love affair that is larger than life, filled with excitement, adventure, and a touch of drama. With a Leo by your side, love becomes a breathtaking journey where you are cherished, adored, and celebrated like royalty.

## MARRIAGE

Marriage with a Leo is a journey of passion, ambition, and the pursuit of greatness. Leos enter into matrimony with a desire to be in charge and make their mark on the world. Their strong-willed nature and unwavering determination can both captivate and challenge their partner.

In the realm of marriage, a Leo demands admiration, respect, and unwavering loyalty. They thrive on being the center of attention, desiring a partner who recognizes their greatness and supports their dreams. They need to be admired, both in public and behind closed doors, and expect their spouse to stand by their side as they conquer the world.

A Leo marriage is far from ordinary. Their larger-than-life personality and magnetic charm bring a touch of grandeur to every aspect of their union. They create an environment that is vibrant, exciting, and filled with passion. With their unwavering commitment, they strive to keep the flames of love and desire burning bright, never allowing the spark to fade.

Leo women in marriage seek admiration and adoration from their partner. They radiate confidence and strength, elevating their spouse and supporting their professional endeavors. They take pride in their role as wives and mothers, balancing their own ambitions with the dedication and care they provide to their family. Their unwavering loyalty and regal presence create a sense of stability and security within the marital bond.

Leo men, on the other hand, may display a more traditional approach to marriage. They appreciate meekness and respect, seeking a partner who embraces their dominant nature. While they may have a tendency to be authoritative, their affectionate nature and desire to treat their spouse like royalty ensure that their marriage remains a grand love affair. They take pride in providing for their family and showering their loved ones with generosity and adoration.

A Leo marriage is not without its challenges. Their need for control and admiration can sometimes border on egoistic, leading to conflicts and power struggles. Both partners must learn to navigate the delicate balance between appreciating Leo's confident nature and ensuring their own needs and desires are met within the relationship.

Yet, beneath their regal exterior, Leo harbors a deep love and devotion for their partner. They are fiercely protective and dedicated, willing to go to great lengths to create a loving and nurturing home environment. They value commitment and loyalty, seeing marriage as a sacred bond that should be cherished and honored.

In a Leo marriage, every day feels like a celebration. From candlelit dinners to surprise getaways, they infuse their union with romance, excitement, and a touch of drama. Their passion is palpable, and their love is an expression of their wholehearted devotion.

Marriage with a Leo is an adventure, a journey where love, passion, and ambition intertwine. It's a partnership where both individuals are encouraged to shine and reach for the stars. With a Leo as your spouse, you embark on a royal bond, where love reigns supreme and dreams are realized in the warmth of their affectionate embrace.

CHAPTER TWO

# LEO 2024 HOROSCOPE

## Overview Leo 2024

Leo, the year 2024 will be a year of significant transformation and growth for you. The planetary movements throughout the year indicate a time of opportunities and challenges that will shape your life in profound ways. The alignment of the Sun, Mercury, Venus, Mars, and Jupiter will play a crucial role in various aspects of your life, including your career, relationships, health, and personal development. Let's delve deeper into what the year has in store for you.

The year 2024 will be a dynamic year for your career. The Sun's opposition to Jupiter in December suggests a time of expansion and growth in your professional life. You may find yourself taking on new responsibilities or stepping into a leadership role.

However, this growth will not come without its challenges. The square between Mercury and Saturn in November indicates potential obstacles that will require careful planning and decision-making. You may need to make tough decisions or navigate difficult conversations at work. However, these challenges will ultimately lead to growth and development in your career.

Financially, the sextile between Venus and Saturn in November indicates stability and potential growth in your financial situation. This is a good time to invest or save money. However, the square between Venus and Uranus in August suggests potential unexpected expenses or financial changes. It's important to be prepared for these potential fluctuations and to manage your finances wisely.

In terms of relationships and social life, the opposition between Venus and Mars in July suggests potential conflicts or disagreements in your personal relationships. These conflicts may stem from differences in values or desires. However, these challenges will provide opportunities for growth and understanding. It's a time to practice patience and empathy and to work on improving your communication skills.

The square between Venus and Neptune in June indicates a time of confusion or misunderstanding in your relationships. You may find yourself questioning your relationships or feeling unsure about your feelings. It's important to communicate clearly and honestly during this time and to seek clarity when needed.

The sesquiquadrate between the Sun and Chiron in June suggests a time of healing and recovery in terms of your health. This is a good time to focus on self-care and wellness practices. You may find yourself drawn to healing modalities such as yoga, meditation, or therapy. The trine between the Sun and Mars in July indicates a period of high energy and vitality. This is a great time to engage in physical activities or to start a new fitness regimen.

The year 2024 will be a significant year for your spiritual growth and personal development. The conjunction between Venus and Pluto in July suggests a time of deep transformation and personal growth. You may find yourself questioning your beliefs or values and seeking deeper meaning in your life. This is a time to embrace change and to allow yourself to grow and evolve.

The sesquiquadrate between Jupiter and Pluto in August indicates a time of spiritual awakening and understanding. You may find yourself drawn to spiritual practices or philosophies that help you understand the world and your place in it. This is a time to explore your spirituality and to seek wisdom and understanding.

The sextile between the Sun and the True Node in July suggests a time of personal development and self-discovery. This is a time to explore your passions and interests and to pursue your personal goals. It's a time to embrace your individuality and to express your true self.

In conclusion, Leo, the year 2024 will be a year of growth, transformation, and self-discovery. While there will be challenges along the way, these challenges will provide opportunities for personal development and understanding. Embrace the journey and make the most of the opportunities that come your way.

# January 2024

### Horoscope

In January 2024, Leo, you will experience a mix of celestial energies that will influence various aspects of your life. The planetary aspects indicate a dynamic and transformative month ahead. It's a time for growth, self-reflection, and taking charge of your destiny.

The month kicks off with a square aspect between Venus in Sagittarius and Saturn in Pisces on January 1st. This alignment may bring some challenges in your relationships and require you to establish stronger boundaries. It's important to communicate openly and honestly with your loved ones during this time.

### Love

Leo, when it comes to matters of the heart, January will be a month of introspection and evaluation. Venus in Sagittarius forms a square aspect with Saturn in Pisces on January 1st, which could create tension in your romantic relationships. It's crucial to address any issues that arise with maturity and understanding.

As the month progresses, Venus forms a quincunx aspect with Jupiter in Taurus on January 3rd, indicating a need for balance and compromise in your love life. Take the time to understand your partner's perspective and find common ground.

For single Leos, this is a time of self-discovery and reflection. Use this period to explore your own desires and values, so you can attract a partner who aligns with your true self.

Career

Leo, January brings a mix of opportunities and challenges in your professional life. The quintile aspect between Mercury and Saturn on January 3rd indicates a time of creative problem-solving and strategic thinking. You have the ability to overcome obstacles and find innovative solutions.

However, be mindful of the square aspect between Mercury in Sagittarius and Neptune in Pisces on January 8th, as it may bring some confusion or miscommunication in your work environment. Stay focused, double-check details, and maintain clear lines of communication to avoid any misunderstandings.

This month also holds the potential for significant career advancements, as Mars forms a trine with Jupiter on January 12th. Your confidence and assertiveness will be key to seizing new opportunities and making progress toward your professional goals. Trust your abilities and take bold steps forward.

Finance

Leo, your financial outlook for January appears stable and promising. With Venus biquintile Jupiter on January 8th, you may experience a stroke of luck or a positive financial opportunity. This alignment encourages you to embrace abundance and make wise financial decisions.

However, it's essential to remain cautious and avoid impulsive spending, especially as Venus forms a semi-square with Pluto on January 10th. Maintain a balanced approach to your finances and consider long-term goals before making any major investments or purchases.

This month is also an ideal time to review your budget and financial plans. Seek professional advice if needed and explore ways to enhance your financial security. By taking a proactive approach, you can strengthen your financial foundation and set yourself up for long-term success.

### Health

Leo, your well-being is a top priority in January. The Sun's square aspect with Chiron on January 6th may bring up emotional wounds or past traumas that require healing. It's crucial to prioritize self-care and seek support from loved ones or professionals if needed.

To maintain your physical health, it's recommended to engage in regular exercise and follow a balanced diet. This month, Mars forms a sextile with Saturn on January 9th, providing you with the discipline and determination needed to establish healthy habits.

Incorporate stress-management techniques into your routine, such as meditation, deep breathing exercises, or engaging in activities you enjoy. Finding a healthy balance between work and relaxation is essential for your overall well-being.

### Travel

Leo, January presents opportunities for travel and exploration. While international travel may still have some restrictions, you can consider local or domestic trips to satisfy your wanderlust.

With the Sun's trine aspect to Uranus on January 9th, spontaneous and unique travel experiences may come your way. Embrace the unexpected and allow yourself to venture outside of your comfort zone.

If travel is not feasible this month, you can explore alternative ways to broaden your horizons, such as learning about different cultures, trying new cuisines, or connecting with people from diverse backgrounds. These experiences can provide valuable insights and expand your perspective.

### Insight from the stars

The astrological aspects in January indicate a month of growth, self-reflection, and transformation for Leo. It's a time to address relationship dynamics, focus on career advancements, and make sound financial decisions. Taking care of your physical and emotional well-being is crucial during this period. Embrace opportunities for travel and exploration, whether near or far. Remember to trust your intuition and stay connected to your inner wisdom. The stars support your journey toward personal growth and fulfillment.

Best days of the month: January 3rd, 9th, 12th, 15th, 19th, 28th and 29th.

# February 2024

## Horoscope

February brings a combination of celestial energies that will shape your path, Leo. It's a month of introspection, emotional growth, and finding balance in various aspects of your life. The planetary aspects encourage self-reflection and offer opportunities for personal transformation. Financial stability is important, so be mindful of spending habits. Take care of your physical and mental well-being through self-care practices. Embrace opportunities for travel and exploration to expand your horizons. The stars guide you towards personal growth and fulfillment.

## Love

Leo, your love life in February will be influenced by deep emotions and a desire for meaningful connections. The square aspect between Venus in Capricorn and Chiron in Aries on February 5th may bring up vulnerabilities and wounds in your relationships. It's essential to approach these issues with compassion and open communication.

As the month progresses, the sextile aspect between Venus and Mars on February 22nd enhances your romantic energy, igniting passion and intensity in your relationships. This alignment encourages you to express your desires and nurture the emotional connection with your partner.

For single Leos, this month offers opportunities for new connections and deepening friendships. Embrace social events and engage in activities that align with your passions and values. By being true to yourself, you'll attract authentic and fulfilling love into your life.

Career

Leo, February presents opportunities for growth and advancement in your professional life. The conjunction between Mercury and Saturn on February 28th empowers you to think strategically and make well-informed decisions. Your focus and determination will help you overcome challenges and achieve your goals.

However, be mindful of the square aspect between Mars and Jupiter on February 27th, as it may bring some tensions or power struggles in the workplace.

Stay calm and diplomatic in your interactions, and focus on finding common ground to resolve conflicts.

This month, it's essential to stay organized, communicate clearly, and leverage your natural leadership abilities. Trust your instincts and take calculated risks when necessary. Your hard work and dedication will lead to recognition and success in your career.

### Finances

Leo, your financial stability is a key focus in February. The semi-square aspect between Venus and Saturn on February 23rd reminds you to be mindful of your spending habits and take a disciplined approach to your finances. It's important to create a realistic budget and stick to it to maintain stability.

The sextile aspect between Venus and Neptune on February 13th brings a touch of inspiration and creativity to your financial decisions. Consider exploring new income streams or investment opportunities that align with your passions and values.

This month is also an ideal time to review your long-term financial plans and seek professional advice if needed. Stay open to innovative approaches and be willing to adapt your strategies to optimize your financial growth and security.

### Health

Leo, taking care of your physical and emotional well-being is crucial in February. The conjunction between the Sun and Mercury on February 28th highlights the importance of balancing your mind and body. Pay attention to your mental health and engage in activities that promote relaxation and inner peace.

It's essential to listen to your body's needs and establish a self-care routine that includes regular exercise, nutritious meals, and sufficient rest. The semi-square aspect between Mars and Neptune on February 24th reminds you to be mindful of your energy levels and avoid overexertion.

This month, prioritize stress management techniques such as meditation, yoga, or engaging in hobbies that bring you joy and fulfillment. Surround yourself with a supportive network of friends and loved ones who uplift and encourage you on your wellness journey.

### Travel

Leo, February offers opportunities for travel and exploration, whether near or far. With the Sun's quintile aspect to Uranus on February 26th, you may feel a desire for spontaneity and adventure. Embrace opportunities to visit new places, experience different cultures, or engage in outdoor activities that ignite your sense of wonder.

If long-distance travel is not feasible, consider exploring your local surroundings and discovering hidden gems in your own backyard. Engage in day trips, weekend getaways, or visit places you've always wanted to explore. The key is to break free from your routine and seek new experiences that expand your horizons.

### Insight from the stars

The celestial energies in February encourage personal growth, emotional healing, and the pursuit of balance in various areas of your life, Leo. It's a month for deepening connections, making strategic career moves, and focusing on financial stability. Prioritize self-care and listen to your body's needs. Embrace opportunities for travel and exploration, be it through physical journeys or expanding your horizons through new experiences. The stars illuminate your path and guide you towards self-discovery and fulfillment.

Best days of the month: February 5th, 13th, 22nd, 26th, 27th and 28th.

## March 2024

Horoscope

March brings a combination of celestial energies that will impact your path, Leo. It's a month of creative inspiration, emotional depth, and self-discovery. The planetary aspects encourage you to embrace your intuition, pursue your passions, and seek balance in various aspects of your life. Relationships, career, finances, and health all require attention and care. Take time for self-reflection and nurture your emotional well-being. March also offers opportunities for exciting travel experiences that broaden your horizons. Trust your instincts and allow the stars to guide you towards personal growth and fulfillment.

Love

Leo, in March, love takes center stage. The sextile aspect between Venus and Chiron on March 6th brings healing and deep emotional connections in your relationships. It's a time to express your feelings openly and embrace vulnerability. Single Leos may find themselves drawn to compassionate and understanding individuals who have the potential for a long-lasting connection. Nurture your relationships through open communication, trust, and acts of kindness. Pay attention to the square aspect between Venus and Uranus on March 3rd, as it may bring some unexpected changes or disruptions in your love life. Embrace these shifts as opportunities for growth and transformation.

Career

March presents opportunities for career advancements and professional growth, Leo. The conjunction between Mercury and Neptune on March 8th enhances your creativity and intuition in the workplace. Trust your instincts and rely on your natural leadership abilities to make strategic decisions. However, be mindful of the square aspect between Mars and Uranus on March 9th, as it may bring some unexpected challenges or disruptions in your professional life. Stay adaptable and approach obstacles with a flexible mindset. Focus on effective communication, collaboration, and problem-solving to overcome any hurdles. With determination and perseverance, you can make significant progress in your career this month.

## Finance

Financial stability is a key focus for Leo in March. The semi-square aspect between Venus and Pluto on March 12th reminds you to be mindful of your financial decisions and avoid impulsive spending. It's important to create a budget, track your expenses, and make wise investments. The sextile aspect between Venus and Jupiter on March 24th brings opportunities for financial growth and abundance. Stay open to new income streams or unexpected financial opportunities that may come your way. Seek advice from trusted financial advisors if needed. Remember to save and invest wisely to secure long-term financial stability.

## Health

In March, taking care of your physical and mental well-being is essential, Leo. The conjunction between the Sun and Neptune on March 17th invites you to prioritize self-care practices and nurture your emotional health. Engage in activities that promote relaxation, such as meditation, yoga, or spending time in nature. The semi-square aspect between Mars and Chiron on March 27th reminds you to pay attention to your energy levels and avoid pushing yourself too hard. Balance physical exercise with sufficient rest and recovery. Listen to your body's needs and make conscious choices that support your overall well-being.

### Travel

March offers opportunities for travel and exploration, Leo. The square aspect between the Sun and Uranus on March 9th ignites your sense of adventure and encourages you to seek new experiences. Whether it's a spontaneous day trip or a planned vacation, embrace the chance to step out of your comfort zone and discover new horizons. Connect with different cultures, try local cuisines, and immerse yourself in new surroundings. If travel is not feasible, explore your local area and uncover hidden gems. Engaging in new experiences and expanding your horizons will provide inspiration and personal growth.

### Insights from the stars

The celestial energies in March emphasize emotional depth, personal growth, and balance, Leo. Trust your intuition, embrace vulnerability, and nurture your relationships. In your career, rely on your instincts and adapt to unexpected changes. Financial stability requires mindful decision-making and wise investments. Take care of your physical and mental well-being through self-care practices. Embrace opportunities for travel and exploration to broaden your horizons. The stars guide you towards emotional healing, creativity, and personal fulfillment.

Best days of the month: March 6th, 9th, 12th, 17th, 24th, 27th and 28th.

# April 2024

## Horoscope

April brings a mix of dynamic energies for you, Leo. It's a month of self-expression, passion, and growth. The celestial aspects inspire you to embrace your individuality, express your creativity, and pursue your passions with vigor. This is a time for personal transformation and stepping into your power. However, be mindful of the need for balance and avoiding impulsive decisions. Nurture your relationships, maintain focus in your career, and pay attention to your financial well-being. Take care of your physical and mental health through self-care practices. Travel opportunities may arise, providing a chance for adventure and new experiences. Trust the wisdom of the stars as you navigate April's energies.

## Love

Leo, love takes center stage in April. The conjunction between Venus and Chiron on April 21st opens the door for deep emotional connections and healing in your relationships. This is a time for forgiveness, compassion, and understanding. Single Leos may find themselves drawn to partners who reflect their own strength and authenticity. Embrace vulnerability and communicate your needs openly. However, be cautious of the semi-square aspect between Venus and Uranus on April 10th, which may bring unexpected changes or disruptions in your love life. Embrace these shifts as opportunities for growth and trust in the transformative power of love.

Career

April brings opportunities for career advancement and professional growth, Leo. The sextile aspect between Mars and Jupiter on April 19th boosts your confidence and ambition. This is a favorable time to take bold action, set new goals, and pursue your career aspirations. However, the semi-square aspect between Mercury and Mars on April 6th advises caution in communication and decision-making. Choose your words carefully and consider the impact of your actions on others. Maintain a balanced approach to work, avoiding impulsiveness or overextending yourself. Seek collaboration and be open to new ideas that can propel your career forward.

## Finance

Financial stability and mindful decision-making are key focuses for Leo in April. The conjunction between Venus and Neptune on April 3rd encourages you to trust your intuition in financial matters. However, be cautious of the semi-square aspect between Venus and Saturn on April 30th, which reminds you to exercise caution and avoid unnecessary risks. Stick to your budget, make wise investments, and seek professional advice if needed. April presents opportunities for financial growth, but it requires careful planning and discipline. Stay focused on long-term stability and resist impulsive spending. Patience and a strategic approach will lead to financial success.

## Health

In April, taking care of your physical and mental well-being is essential, Leo. The conjunction between Mars and Neptune on April 29th reminds you to pay attention to your energy levels and emotional boundaries. Practice self-care routines that rejuvenate your body and nourish your soul. Incorporate activities such as yoga, meditation, or spending time in nature to promote relaxation and inner balance. Be mindful of the semi-square aspect between the Sun and Saturn on April 2nd, which may bring temporary dips in energy or feelings of fatigue. Listen to your body's needs, prioritize rest, and seek emotional support when necessary. Balance work and play to maintain overall health and well-being.

Travel

April offers opportunities for travel and exploration, Leo. The conjunction between Venus and Chiron on April 21st inspires you to seek new experiences and expand your horizons. Whether it's a spontaneous day trip or a planned getaway, embrace the chance to discover new cultures, cuisines, and landscapes. Traveling solo or with loved ones can deepen your connections and provide valuable insights. However, be mindful of the semi-square aspect between Venus and Saturn on April 13th, which may require careful planning and budgeting for travel expenses. Prepare well in advance and consider practical aspects such as accommodations and transportation. Embrace the sense of adventure and embrace the world with an open heart and mind.

Insight from the stars

The celestial alignments in April guide you towards personal growth, emotional healing, and expressing your authentic self. Trust in the transformative power of love, embrace opportunities for career advancement, and make wise financial decisions. Nurture your physical and mental health through self-care practices and balance work with relaxation. Explore new horizons through travel and stay open to the lessons and experiences that await you. The stars remind you of your inner strength and encourage you to step into your power, allowing your light to shine brightly.

Best days of the month: April 4th, 8th, 11th, 15th, 19th, 22nd, and 25th

## May 2024

Horoscope

May is a month of profound significance for you, Leo. As the Sun continues its journey through Taurus, it illuminates your sector of self-expression, creativity, and personal growth. The celestial energies this month beckon you to embrace your inner fire, unleash your passions, and step into your power with unwavering confidence. It's a time of profound transformation and a call to honor your authentic self.

The conjunction between Venus and Uranus on May 18th ignites a spark of excitement and brings unexpected encounters in your romantic life. This cosmic alignment encourages you to break free from conventional patterns and explore new connections. Single Leos may find themselves drawn to unique and unconventional partners, while those in committed relationships may experience a revitalization of love and an infusion of electrifying energy. However, be cautious of the semi-square aspect between Venus and Mars on May 29th, as it may bring tension or conflicts in relationships. Open and honest communication is essential to maintain harmony during this time.

In summary, May is a transformative month for you, Leo. Embrace your authentic self, follow your heart's desires, and trust in the journey. The celestial energies support your personal growth, love life, career aspirations, financial stability, health, and travel endeavors. Allow yourself to be guided by the stars as you navigate the profound energies of May, and remember that you have the power to shape your destiny and manifest your dreams.

Love

Leo, love takes center stage in May. The conjunction between Venus and Uranus on May 18th brings excitement and unexpected encounters in your romantic life. This is a time for exploring new connections, embracing spontaneity, and breaking free from conventional patterns. Single Leos may find themselves drawn to unique and unconventional partners. However, be cautious of the semi-square aspect between Venus and Mars on May 29th, which may bring tension or conflicts. Practice open and honest communication to maintain harmony in your relationships. Embrace the adventurous and unpredictable nature of love, and trust that the right connections will unfold.

### Career

May brings opportunities for career growth and professional development, Leo. The sextile aspect between Mars and Pluto on May 3rd empowers you with determination and the ability to overcome obstacles. This is a favorable time to assert your ambitions, take on new challenges, and make progress in your career. However, be mindful of the square aspect between Mercury and Pluto on May 17th, which advises caution in communication and decision-making. Choose your words wisely and avoid power struggles. Seek collaborations and networking opportunities that can enhance your professional journey. Embrace your leadership skills and trust in your abilities to achieve success.

### Finance

Financial stability and strategic planning are key focuses for Leo in May. The conjunction between Venus and Jupiter on May 23rd brings opportunities for abundance and financial growth. This is a time to expand your financial horizons and seek new avenues for income. However, be cautious of the semi-square aspect between Venus and Neptune on May 10th, which may cloud your judgment or lead to impulsive spending. Maintain a balanced approach to money management and avoid risky investments. Set realistic financial goals and stick to your budget. Seek professional advice if needed and trust your instincts when making financial decisions.

### Health

In May, prioritizing your physical and mental well-being is crucial, Leo. The semi-square aspect between the Sun and Neptune on May 3rd reminds you to maintain healthy boundaries and be mindful of your energy levels. Practice self-care routines that rejuvenate your body and nurture your soul. Regular exercise, proper nutrition, and sufficient rest are essential for maintaining your vitality. Be cautious of overextending yourself or taking on too many responsibilities. Seek support from loved ones and incorporate stress-management techniques into your daily routine. Embrace relaxation practices such as meditation or spending time in nature to foster inner balance and overall well-being.

### Travel

May presents opportunities for travel and exploration, Leo. The conjunction between Venus and Uranus on May 18th ignites your sense of adventure and encourages you to embrace spontaneity. This is a favorable time to plan a getaway or embark on a journey of self-discovery. Open yourself up to new cultures, experiences, and perspectives. However, be mindful of practical considerations and plan your travels carefully to ensure smooth experiences. Embrace the freedom and inspiration that travel brings and allow yourself to step out of your comfort zone. Whether it's a solo adventure or a shared experience with loved ones, May offers a chance to create lasting memories and broaden your horizons.

### Insight from the stars

May brings a powerful energy of transformation and growth for Leo. Trust in your intuition and follow your heart's desires. Embrace change, be open to new experiences, and allow your authentic self to shine. This month encourages you to step into your personal power and pursue your passions with confidence. Remember to maintain balance, practice open communication, and prioritize self-care. The stars remind you of your inherent strength and guide you towards a path of self-discovery and fulfillment. Trust in the journey and embrace the transformative energies that May brings.

Best days of the month: May 7th, 11th, 15th, 18th, 21st, 25th and 30th

# June 2024

## Horoscope

Dear Leo, get ready for an exciting and transformative month ahead! The cosmic energies are conspiring to bring positive changes and opportunities your way. As the Sun moves through Gemini, your sector of communication and self-expression, your words become a powerful tool for manifesting your desires. This is an ideal time to share your ideas, engage in meaningful conversations, and captivate others with your charismatic charm. Embrace the power of your creativity and let your voice be heard. Be open to new experiences and embrace the winds of change that are blowing in your favor.

## Love

In matters of the heart, June brings passion, intensity, and a dash of unpredictability. The sextile aspect between the Sun and True Node on June 3rd ignites the flames of romance, bringing deep emotional connections and exciting encounters. Single Leos may find themselves drawn to magnetic and captivating individuals who awaken their desires. However, be cautious of the square aspect between Venus and Neptune on June 8th, which may create confusion or illusions in relationships. Honesty, transparency, and open communication are key to navigating these challenges and maintaining harmonious connections. Dive deep into your emotions, express your true feelings, and forge bonds based on trust and authenticity.

Career

This month, the spotlight shines brightly on your professional endeavors, dear Leo. The trine aspect between Mercury and Saturn on June 19th empowers you with focus, discipline, and strategic thinking. Your ability to communicate your ideas with precision and gather support from colleagues and superiors is at its peak. Take advantage of this favorable energy to pursue new responsibilities, engage in negotiations, or embark on entrepreneurial ventures. The conjunction between Mercury and Venus on June 14th brings favorable collaborations and partnerships that can lead to success and fulfillment. However, be mindful of the square aspect between Mercury and Chiron on June

28th, which may temporarily challenge your confidence and decision-making. Trust in your abilities, seek guidance when needed, and stay committed to your long-term goals.

### Finance

June presents a mixed financial outlook for you, dear Leo. The square aspect between Venus and Saturn on June 8th advises caution in monetary matters. It's crucial to practice prudent budgeting, avoid impulsive spending, and focus on long-term financial stability. Seek professional advice and conduct thorough research before making any major investments or financial decisions. However, the sextile aspect between Venus and Mars on June 29th brings the potential for financial gains through joint ventures or collaborations. Stay open to partnerships that align with your values and long-term goals. Harness your natural charisma and negotiation skills to secure favorable deals and advantageous financial opportunities.

### Health

Taking care of your well-being becomes paramount in June, dear Leo. The Sun's quintile aspect with Neptune on June 1st encourages you to explore holistic practices, meditation, or spiritual pursuits that enhance your emotional and mental well-being. Find balance between your work commitments and personal life, ensuring that you prioritize self-care routines. Engaging in physical activities that bring you joy and help release stress is highly beneficial. Pay attention to your emotional needs and seek support from loved ones or professionals if necessary. Remember to take time for yourself, allowing moments of solitude to recharge and rejuvenate your energy.

### Travel

June invites you to embark on exciting journeys and explore new horizons, dear Leo. The conjunction between Mercury and Jupiter on June 4th sparks your curiosity and ignites a thirst for fresh experiences. Plan short trips or getaways that broaden your horizons and offer a change of scenery. Whether it's a solo adventure or quality time spent with loved ones, embrace the opportunity to create lasting memories and gain fresh insights. Traveling can also open doors to valuable networking opportunities and expand your professional connections. Keep an open mind, be receptive to different cultures, and allow yourself to be immersed in the beauty and diversity of the world.

Insight from the stars

The celestial alignments in June empower you, dear Leo, to embrace change, express your creativity, and nurture your relationships. It's a month where your words carry immense power, allowing you to captivate others with your charm and influence. Trust your intuition and let your passion guide you in matters of the heart. In your career, focus on effective communication, strategic thinking, and forging alliances that support your ambitions. Nurture your well-being and make self-care a priority. Embrace the adventures that travel brings and let it expand your horizons. Remember, the stars are aligned in your favor, so seize the opportunities that come your way!

Best days of the month: June 4th, 8th, 14th, 19th, 22nd, 28th and 29th.

# July 2024

## Horoscope

In July, Leo, you are set to experience a dynamic and transformative period. The alignment of Jupiter in Gemini and Chiron in Aries suggests that you will be challenged to confront any deep-rooted insecurities and wounds that may have hindered your personal growth. This is an opportunity for healing and growth, allowing you to emerge stronger and more self-assured. The presence of Mercury quintile Mars emphasizes effective communication and assertiveness, enabling you to express your ideas and desires with clarity and confidence. However, be cautious of the semi-square between the Sun in Cancer and Uranus in Taurus, which may introduce unexpected disruptions or changes in your plans. Embrace flexibility and adaptability to navigate these challenges successfully.

### Love

Leo, your love life in July is characterized by emotional intensity and transformation. The trine between Venus in Cancer and Saturn in Pisces indicates stability and commitment in your relationships. This is an excellent time for deepening emotional bonds and building a solid foundation. However, the square between Venus and Chiron may bring up unresolved emotional wounds, requiring honest communication and vulnerability with your partner. Use this opportunity to heal and strengthen your connection. Single Leos may find themselves drawn to profound and transformative relationships, but it's important to remain true to your authentic self and not compromise your values.

### Career

July presents promising opportunities for your career, Leo. The sextile between Mercury and Jupiter enhances your communication skills and intellectual abilities, allowing you to articulate your ideas with confidence and enthusiasm. This can lead to new collaborations, favorable negotiations, and successful presentations. The trine between Mercury and the True Node suggests that your ideas and actions align with your long-term goals and aspirations, bringing recognition and advancement. However, be mindful of the sesquiquadrate aspect between Mercury and Neptune, which may introduce some confusion or deceptive influences. Trust your intuition and seek clarity to make informed decisions.

Finance

Leo, your financial outlook in July is stable and secure. The trine between Venus and Saturn indicates a disciplined and responsible approach to money matters. This is a favorable time for long-term financial planning, investments, and savings. The semi-square between the Sun and Jupiter suggests the need for moderation and caution, avoiding overspending or impulsive financial decisions. Stay focused on your financial goals and resist the temptation to indulge in unnecessary expenses. Practicing financial prudence will ensure stability and future growth.

Health

In terms of health, July highlights the importance of self-care and emotional well-being, Leo. The square between the Sun and Chiron may bring up unresolved emotional issues or physical discomfort. Take time to nurture yourself and address any lingering health concerns. Incorporating activities that promote relaxation and stress relief, such as meditation or gentle exercise, can greatly benefit your overall well-being. Remember to listen to your body's needs and seek professional guidance if necessary. Prioritizing self-care will help you maintain balance and vitality throughout the month.

Travel

July presents opportunities for exciting and enriching travel experiences, Leo. The sextile between Mars and Neptune infuses your adventures with inspiration, creativity, and a sense of adventure. Whether you embark on a spontaneous weekend getaway or a well-planned international trip, you'll find joy and personal growth through exploration. Embrace new cultures, immerse yourself in different environments, and open yourself up to unexpected encounters. Traveling can broaden your perspective and offer fresh insights, allowing you to return home with a renewed sense of purpose.

Insights from the stars

The celestial alignment in July urges you, Leo, to embrace change and transformation. The presence of Jupiter and Chiron signifies a period of growth and healing, offering you the opportunity to confront and overcome deep-seated fears or insecurities. Trust in your ability to navigate challenges and have faith in your own resilience. This transformative energy will shape your personal and professional life, providing the foundation for long-lasting success and fulfillment. Embrace the guidance of the stars and embrace the opportunities that lie ahead.

Best days of the month: July 2nd, 8th, 11th, 15th, 19th, 21st, 31st.

# August 2024

Horoscope

Leo, the month of August brings a mix of dynamic energy and transformative opportunities for you. With Mars sextile True Node, you'll have the drive and determination to pursue your goals and align your actions with your long-term aspirations. However, the semi-square between Mars and Chiron may bring up some insecurities or wounds that need healing. It's essential to confront these challenges and work on personal growth. The quintile aspect between Venus and Jupiter enhances your charm and social interactions, attracting positive experiences and expanding your connections. However, be cautious of the square between Venus and Uranus, which may introduce unexpected changes or disruptions in your relationships. Embrace adaptability and open-mindedness to navigate these shifts successfully.

### Love

In matters of the heart, August offers Leo an opportunity for growth and deepening connections. The biquintile between Venus and Jupiter enhances your romantic charisma, making you more alluring and captivating to potential partners. It's a favorable time for passionate encounters and meaningful connections. However, the quincunx aspect between Venus and Neptune may introduce some confusion or unrealistic expectations. Ensure open and honest communication to avoid misunderstandings and maintain the harmony in your relationships. For committed Leos, this is a time to nurture and strengthen the emotional bond with your partner, supporting each other's growth and aspirations.

### Career

Leo, your professional life in August is marked by assertiveness and determination. The biquintile between Sun and Saturn empowers you to take charge of your career and make progress toward your goals. Your leadership skills and ability to handle responsibilities shine brightly during this time. The conjunction of Mercury and Venus brings effective communication and negotiation skills, making it an ideal period for collaboration and successful partnerships. However, be mindful of the square between Sun and Uranus, which may introduce unexpected changes or disruptions in your professional plans. Embrace flexibility and adaptability to navigate these challenges and turn them into opportunities for growth.

Finance

August presents a stable and secure financial outlook for Leo. The trine between Venus and Uranus brings unexpected financial opportunities and innovative ideas for generating income. You may encounter new investment prospects or unconventional sources of revenue. However, the quincunx aspect between Sun and Saturn cautions against impulsive financial decisions. Maintain a balanced approach, carefully evaluating risks and rewards before making any significant financial commitments. Focus on long-term financial stability and engage in prudent financial planning to secure your future.

### Health

In terms of health, August reminds Leo to prioritize self-care and emotional well-being. The sesquiquadrate aspect between Sun and Neptune suggests the need for balance and relaxation. Pay attention to your mental and emotional health, ensuring adequate rest and stress management. Engage in activities that promote relaxation and rejuvenation, such as meditation, yoga, or spending time in nature. Nurturing your emotional well-being will enhance your overall vitality and enable you to approach life with renewed energy and enthusiasm.

### Travel

Leo, August offers exciting opportunities for travel and exploration. The quintile aspect between Mars and Neptune infuses your adventures with creativity, inspiration, and a sense of adventure. Whether it's a spontaneous weekend getaway or a well-planned vacation, embrace the opportunity to immerse yourself in new cultures, environments, and experiences. Traveling during this period will broaden your horizons, stimulate your mind, and provide valuable insights. Embrace the unknown and make the most of the transformative power of travel.

Insight from the stars

The celestial alignment in August emphasizes the need for personal growth and transformation, Leo. The presence of Jupiter and Pluto urges you to confront deep-seated fears or insecurities, allowing for profound personal development. This is a time to break free from limiting beliefs and embrace your true potential. The quintile between Jupiter and the True Node indicates that aligning your actions with your life's purpose will lead to favorable outcomes and spiritual growth. Trust in the wisdom of the stars and embrace the transformative energy that surrounds you.

Best days of the month: August 2nd, 6th, 15th, 22nd, 23rd, 27th, and 30th.

## September 2024

### Horoscope

Leo, September brings a period of self-reflection, communication, and opportunities for personal growth. With the trine aspect between Mercury and Chiron, you are encouraged to explore and heal emotional wounds, fostering greater self-awareness and understanding. This is a favorable time for introspection and engaging in conversations that promote emotional healing. The quintile aspect between Sun and Mars enhances your energy, motivation, and assertiveness, enabling you to take action towards your goals. However, be mindful of the square between Mars and Neptune, which may introduce some confusion or lack of clarity. It's essential to stay grounded and trust your intuition to navigate these challenges successfully.

Love

In matters of the heart, September presents Leo with opportunities for deep connections and emotional growth. The opposition between Venus and True Node may bring some tension or contrasting desires within your relationships. It's crucial to find a balance between your personal needs and the expectations of your partner. Open and honest communication will be the key to maintaining harmony and finding resolutions. The sesquiquadrate aspect between Venus and Jupiter suggests the need for moderation and balance in love and relationships. Take the time to nurture and appreciate the emotional bond you share with your partner, fostering trust and mutual understanding.

Career

September brings positive developments and growth in your professional life, Leo. The trine between Sun and Uranus opens doors to new opportunities and innovative ideas in your career. Embrace change and be open to unconventional approaches that can lead to success. The square aspect between Mercury and Jupiter brings a boost to your communication and negotiation skills, making it an excellent time for collaborations, networking, and expanding your professional connections. However, be cautious of the quincunx between Mercury and Chiron, which may introduce some challenges or miscommunications. Stay patient, listen attentively, and clarify any misunderstandings to maintain smooth professional relationships.

Finance

Leo, September presents a favorable financial outlook with opportunities for stability and growth. The trine aspect between Mercury and Pluto enhances your financial acumen, allowing you to make insightful decisions and strategize effectively. This is a time to focus on long-term financial planning and investment opportunities that can yield fruitful results. However, the opposition between Venus and Saturn cautions against impulsive spending or risky financial ventures. Practice prudence and disciplined budgeting to maintain financial stability and ensure future prosperity.

### Health

In terms of health, September reminds Leo to prioritize self-care and balance. The sesquiquadrate aspect between Sun and Pluto suggests the need for moderation and avoiding extremes. Maintain a balanced approach to your well-being, focusing on both physical and emotional health. Engage in regular exercise, eat nourishing foods, and practice mindfulness to foster overall vitality and mental clarity. It's also essential to manage stress and create space for relaxation and rejuvenation. Taking care of your well-being will allow you to approach challenges with resilience and maintain optimal health.

### Travel

Leo, September offers opportunities for travel and exploration that will broaden your horizons and stimulate personal growth. The biquintile aspect between Venus and Neptune infuses your journeys with inspiration, creativity, and a sense of adventure. Whether it's a spontaneous trip or a well-planned vacation, embrace the opportunity to immerse yourself in new cultures, experiences, and environments. Travel will provide valuable insights, broaden your perspective, and allow for personal transformation.

Embrace the unknown and make the most of the transformative power of travel.

### Insight from the stars

The celestial alignment in September encourages Leo to focus on personal growth, self-reflection, and effective communication. The trine between Mercury and Chiron urges you to confront emotional wounds and engage in healing conversations that promote self-awareness and understanding. Trust your intuition and navigate any challenges with grace and resilience. The quintile aspect between Sun and Mars infuses you with energy, motivation, and assertiveness, enabling you to take confident steps towards your goals. Embrace change, maintain balance in relationships, and approach both personal and professional matters with a balanced perspective.

Best days of the month: September 2nd, 10th, 12th, 15th, 19th, 25th and 30th.

## October 2024

### Horoscope

Leo, October brings a transformative and introspective energy as you delve deep into your emotions and relationships. With the sesquiquadrate aspect between Mercury and Uranus, you may experience some unexpected changes or disruptions in communication. It's important to stay adaptable and open-minded to navigate these shifts successfully. The trine aspect between Venus and Saturn fosters stability and commitment in your love life, encouraging deeper emotional connections. This month is a time for self-reflection, emotional healing, and embracing your passions. Trust your intuition and be open to the transformative power of love and self-discovery.

### Love

In matters of the heart, October brings a mix of intensity and stability for Leo. The trine between Venus and Saturn emphasizes commitment and deep emotional bonds. It's a time for nurturing and strengthening relationships, focusing on long-term stability and shared goals. The square aspect between Venus and Uranus may introduce some unexpected challenges or disruptions in your love life. It's important to embrace change and approach conflicts with open communication and a willingness to compromise. This month offers opportunities for growth, increased emotional depth, and the potential for a more profound connection with your partner.

Career

October presents Leo with opportunities for growth and advancement in their professional life. The square aspect between Mercury and Mars may bring some challenges or conflicts in the workplace. It's crucial to maintain a diplomatic approach, prioritize effective communication, and find constructive solutions to overcome any obstacles. The trine aspect between Mercury and Jupiter enhances your communication skills, making it an excellent time for negotiations, presentations, and collaborations. Embrace your natural leadership abilities, trust your instincts, and be open to innovative ideas that can propel your career forward.

### Finance

In terms of finances, October calls for prudence and careful decision-making for Leo. The opposition between Sun and Pluto may introduce power struggles or financial challenges. It's crucial to avoid impulsive spending and instead focus on long-term financial stability and security. The trine aspect between Venus and Mars encourages financial harmony and the potential for increased income through collaboration or joint ventures. Seek opportunities for financial growth that align with your long-term goals and maintain disciplined budgeting practices to ensure financial stability.

### Health

October highlights the importance of self-care and emotional well-being for Leo. The sesquiquadrate aspect between Sun and Neptune may bring some confusion or lack of clarity regarding your health and well-being. It's crucial to prioritize self-care routines, set healthy boundaries, and practice stress management techniques. Nurturing your emotional health is equally important, so make time for self-reflection, relaxation, and activities that bring you joy. Pay attention to your intuition and listen to your body's needs, ensuring that you take the necessary steps to maintain overall wellness.

Travel

Leo, October presents opportunities for transformative travel experiences that broaden your horizons and provide personal growth. The biquintile aspect between Mercury and Neptune enhances your travel experiences with inspiration, creativity, and a sense of adventure. Embrace the unknown, explore new cultures, and engage in meaningful connections during your journeys. Travel can be a powerful catalyst for personal transformation and self-discovery. Whether it's a spiritual retreat or an immersive cultural exploration, allow yourself to be open to the transformative power of travel.

Insight from the stars

The celestial alignment in October encourages Leo to embrace transformation, deep emotional connections, and self-reflection. The trine between Venus and Saturn fosters stability and commitment in love, urging you to prioritize emotional depth and long-term relationships. The trine between Mercury and Jupiter enhances your communication skills and fosters opportunities for growth in your career. However, the square between Mercury and Mars may introduce some conflicts, urging you to find diplomatic solutions. Stay grounded, trust your intuition, and embrace change with grace and resilience.

Best days of the month: October 8th, 12th, 15th, 22nd, 23rd, 28th and 31st.

# November 2024

## Horoscope

Leo, November brings a mix of transformative energy and opportunities for personal growth. With the sextile aspect between Jupiter and Chiron, you are supported in your journey of healing and self-discovery. This month encourages you to explore your beliefs, expand your knowledge, and embrace new experiences. The trine aspect between Mercury and Mars enhances your communication skills and provides you with the courage to express your ideas and opinions. It's a time for taking action, making important decisions, and pursuing your passions. Embrace the transformative energy of November and allow yourself to grow and evolve.

## Love

In matters of the heart, November offers Leo opportunities for growth and deepening connections. The opposition between Venus and Jupiter may introduce some challenges or conflicts in relationships. It's important to maintain open and honest communication to overcome any misunderstandings or differences. The trine aspect between Venus and Chiron supports emotional healing and encourages you to let go of past wounds. This month calls for vulnerability and authenticity in relationships, allowing for deeper emotional intimacy and understanding.

### Career

November brings exciting possibilities and professional growth for Leo. The opposition between Mercury and Jupiter enhances your communication skills and fosters new opportunities in your career. It's a time for networking, negotiations, and collaborations that can propel your professional endeavors forward. The square aspect between Mercury and Saturn may introduce some challenges or delays. It's important to stay focused, disciplined, and patient as you navigate through any obstacles. Trust your instincts, believe in your abilities, and embrace new challenges with confidence.

### Finance

In terms of finances, November encourages Leo to maintain a balanced and disciplined approach. The trine aspect between Venus and Saturn fosters stability and responsible financial management. It's a favorable time for long-term financial planning, investments, and building a solid foundation for your financial future. The square aspect between Venus and Neptune may introduce some financial challenges or temptations. It's important to stay grounded and avoid impulsive decisions. Prioritize financial stability and focus on sustainable growth rather than short-term gains.

### Health

November highlights the importance of self-care and holistic well-being for Leo. The sesquiquadrate aspect between Sun and Neptune may bring some confusion or lack of clarity regarding your health and well-being. It's crucial to prioritize self-care routines, maintain a healthy lifestyle, and establish boundaries to avoid burnout. Pay attention to your emotional and mental health, as they play a significant role in overall well-being. Engage in activities that bring you joy, practice mindfulness, and seek balance in all aspects of your life.

## Travel

Leo, November offers opportunities for meaningful and transformative travel experiences. The biquintile aspect between Venus and Mars enhances your adventurous spirit and fuels your desire for new experiences. Embrace the unknown, explore different cultures, and engage in activities that broaden your horizons. Travel can be a source of inspiration, personal growth, and self-discovery. Whether it's a spiritual retreat, a cultural immersion, or a nature adventure, allow yourself to embrace the transformative power of travel and create lasting memories.

## Insights from the stars

The celestial alignment in November encourages Leo to embrace personal growth, deep emotional connections, and the pursuit of new experiences. The sextile between Jupiter and Chiron supports your journey of healing and self-discovery, urging you to let go of past wounds and embrace new beliefs. The opposition between Venus and Jupiter may introduce some challenges in relationships, calling for open communication and understanding. Trust your instincts, follow your passions, and believe in your ability to create positive change in your life.

Best days of the month: November 2nd, 4th, 9th, 19th, 23rd, 27th and 30th.

## December 2024

Horoscope

Leo, December brings a mix of transformative energy and opportunities for growth. With the biquintile aspect between Venus and Jupiter, you are supported in expanding your horizons, embracing new experiences, and fostering a positive outlook. This month encourages you to tap into your creativity, express your unique self, and pursue your passions with enthusiasm. The opposition between Mercury and Jupiter enhances your communication skills, making it an ideal time for networking, negotiations, and sharing your ideas. Embrace the transformative energy of December and trust in your ability to create positive change in your life.

Love

In matters of the heart, December offers Leo opportunities for deep emotional connections and growth. The trine aspect between Venus and Uranus ignites excitement and spontaneity in relationships. It's a time for exploring new avenues of connection, embracing change, and bringing fresh energy into your love life. The semi-square aspect between Venus and Neptune may introduce some challenges or confusion in relationships. It's important to stay grounded and maintain open communication to overcome any misunderstandings or illusions. Embrace authenticity, nurture emotional intimacy, and allow love to unfold naturally.

Career

December brings promising opportunities and professional growth for Leo. The opposition between Mercury and Jupiter amplifies your communication skills and fosters successful collaborations and negotiations. It's a time for expanding your knowledge, sharing your ideas, and taking calculated risks in your career. The square aspect between Mercury and Saturn may introduce some challenges or delays. It's crucial to stay focused, disciplined, and patient as you navigate through any obstacles. Trust your instincts, maintain a positive mindset, and leverage your skills and expertise to achieve professional success.

### Finance

In terms of finances, December encourages Leo to adopt a practical and disciplined approach. The semi-square aspect between Venus and Saturn emphasizes the importance of responsible financial management and long-term stability. It's a favorable time for budgeting, financial planning, and making informed decisions regarding your resources. The square aspect between Venus and Uranus may introduce some unexpected financial changes or expenses. Stay adaptable and open-minded and seek opportunities for financial growth through innovation and strategic planning.

### Health

December highlights the importance of self-care and maintaining a balanced approach to your well-being. The semi-square aspect between Sun and Venus may bring some challenges or fluctuations in your physical and emotional health. It's important to prioritize self-care routines, maintain a healthy lifestyle, and seek support when needed. Focus on activities that bring you joy and help you find inner harmony. Nurture your emotional well-being, practice mindfulness, and embrace a holistic approach to health.

### Travel

Leo, December offers opportunities for meaningful and transformative travel experiences. The biquintile aspect between Sun and Uranus ignites your sense of adventure and encourages you to explore new destinations and cultures. Embrace spontaneity, step out of your comfort zone, and engage in activities that broaden your horizons. Travel can be a source of inspiration, personal growth, and self-discovery. Whether it's a spiritual retreat, a nature escape, or an immersive cultural experience, allow yourself to embrace the transformative power of travel and create lasting memories.

### Insight from the stars

The celestial alignment in December encourages Leo to embrace personal growth, expand their horizons, and foster meaningful connections. The biquintile aspect between Venus and Jupiter supports your journey of self-discovery and encourages a positive outlook. The opposition between Mercury and

Jupiter enhances your communication skills, empowering you to express your ideas and negotiate successfully. Trust your intuition, believe in your abilities, and tap into your creative potential. December offers opportunities for transformation, love, and professional growth. Embrace the energy of this month and allow it to guide you towards a brighter future.

Best days of the month: December 2nd, 4th, 10th, 18th, 19th, 21st, 31st.

Manufactured by Amazon.ca
Acheson, AB